Why Do You Weep?

Finding Consolation and Peace in Times of Grief

Larry Kaufmann, CSsR

Seán Wales, CSsR

Russell Pollitt, SJ

Liguori

ONE LIGUORI DRIVE
LIGUORI MO 63057-9999

Imprimi Potest:
Harry Grile, CSsR, Provincial
Denver Province, The Redemptorists

Published by Liguori Publications, Liguori, Missouri 63057
To order, call 800-325-9521, or visit liguori.org.

Library of Congress Cataloging-in-Publication Data

Kaufmann, Larry
   Why do you weep? : finding consolation and peace in times of grief /
Larry Kaufmann, Seán Wales, and Russell Pollitt.—1st ed.
     p. cm.
  ISBN 978-0-7648-2077-9
  1. Bereavement—Religious aspects—Catholic Church. 2. Grief—Religious aspects—
Catholic Church. 3. Consolation. I. Wales, Seán. II. Pollitt, Russell. III. Title.
    BX2373.B47K38 2011
    248.8"66—dc23

                                                    2011037347

Liguori Publications, a nonprofit corporation, is an apostolate of the Redemptorists. To learn more about the Redemptorists, visit Redemptorists.com.

Printed in the United States of America
16 15 14 13 12 / 5 4 3 2 1
First Edition

Contents

Preface

The title of this book is taken from the question the angels put to Mary Magdalene as she sought the body of Jesus at the tomb after his crucifixion: "Woman, why are you weeping?" Mary Magdalene's grief was real, and it was deep. As she articulates her grief, the risen Jesus himself comes to her and says, "Mary!"

Jesus also comes to those who mourn the death of the ones they have loved. The reflections and prayers that follow are humble attempts to bring you, the reader, into contact with the compassion of Jesus as you grapple with questions of faith and feelings of loss in the face of death.

Words are ultimately inadequate for the kind of suffering that follows the death of a loved one. Yet despite their limitations they may be able to resonate with something that goes on in the soul as we move through the phases of mourning. That is why the various sections of this book are to be treated more as meditations than as "answers. In meditation we bring our own questions and thoughts into dialogue with the insights and experiences of others.

Thus, as Father Russell Pollitt, SJ, writes about the suicide of his own brother, we may find a kindred spirit who walks with us on our own journey in trying to make sense of our confusion, not necessarily from a death through suicide but from any death that seems absurd. For those who have suffered the loss of a parent, the words of Saint Augustine after the death of his mother, Saint Monica, may strike a chord. When death results from a violent and evil act, it may help to sit for a while in the company of Etty Hillesum and Christian de Chergé, both of whom grappled with the temptation to seek revenge. For parents who lose a child, there are indeed no words that could bring adequate comfort. Yet it may be a consolation for them to be in the company of Mary, the Mother of Jesus, as they, with her, endure the long Holy Saturday that falls between Good Friday and Easter Sunday.

These reflections are offered in love. They come from years of pastoral experience, ministering to those who are bereaved, conducting funerals, leading bereavement retreats during parish missions, and they come from our own experiences, as the writers, also having suffered personal loss and sadness. May the meditations that follow be for you an assurance that you are not alone but are held before God in our prayers and the offering of Mass, both for those who have died and for you and your families who mourn.

Larry Kaufmann, CSsR
Seán Wales, CSsR
Russell Pollitt, SJ

1

Holy Saturday
of Grief

Our hearts are torn open in the experience of the death of a loved one. Whether as a grieving husband, wife, mother, father, son, daughter, brother, sister, cousin, loved one, or friend, we each experience private and shared grief seeking a word of meaning, of hope, of consolation. We wait for a word from God to be spoken into our pain. And the word we have usually heard is...nothing but silence! Indeed, the silence of God.

To enter into the silence—the silence that results from grief—and to stay with that silence, takes us to the very beginning of creation, to the formless, empty void described in the Book of Genesis. And slowly, quietly, and gently during days of grief and loss we begin to hear the soft wings of the Holy Spirit at the dawn of creation, bringing to birth and mothering new life in the midst of darkness and death. Many of the Church's great theologians have spoken about the *creatio ex nihilo* (creation out of nothing). God's Spirit brings life out of the dark void of nothingness.

There is another "silence" we can enter into in the midst

of grief. In the wordlessness of bereavement, we also find ourselves in the dark silent tomb of Holy Saturday, where Jesus was buried after his death. It is a necessary place to be for a while (and only a mourner knows how long that "while" should be, as one of the other reflections in this book points out.) A Christian funeral, in the mind of the Church, is a celebration of the death and resurrection of Christ as we pass with him from our own Good Friday to share in his Easter Sunday. But perhaps we too easily pass over that middle Saturday—the longest day—of silent waiting. Hope needs to bide its time, yet we fail to dwell on that time when Jesus is truly dead among the dead, cut off from the land of the living, gone from this world into eternal silence. To hurry past that Holy Saturday to the triumph of Easter Sunday is to deny the harsh reality of Jesus' death and perhaps our own. Yet without the ability to grieve, we can have no capacity for real hope.

The death of a loved one plunges us into the full meaning of that Holy Saturday, a day of wondering when God will act, a day of feeling the absence of God, a day when all our theories and pious thoughts are silenced. Holy Saturday has been called "the forgotten day." Yet it is an amazing day of destiny. Holy Saturday has also been called "that dark space where the tomb becomes the womb, that uncertain time when the light creeps in."

On Holy Saturday we find ourselves back in the formless, empty void before creation. And in that apparent nothingness, once again we come face to face with the Creator Spirit who is quite at home in voids, working gently and lovingly to create new life, indeed, risen life! In the words of Anthony

Kelly, CSsR, "The dark tomb of Holy Saturday into which all of us must enter with Jesus is a pledge that in and through the wrenching of death—terrible at times—an ever-so-quiet 'Alleluia' can be heard."

The Holy Saturday tomb of Jesus reminds us that among the keynotes of suffering and sorrow there are soft silences where we can come and rest. Only in that silence can we truly hear the words of Jesus: "Peace I leave with you; my peace I give to you....Do not let your hearts be troubled or afraid....I am going away and I will come back to you" (John 14:27, 28).

And as we hear these words, we know that death is, after all, not the end but the beginning of a whole new way of relating in the communion of saints. That is what we believe. True enough, we do not know how that continuity takes place. But our faith professes it to be real. ("I believe in...the communion of saints.") But still we ask: "Where is _____ to be found?" There is only one answer: "No longer in the material world around us. _____ abides in God."

Faced as we are by the ultimate questions of life, we know so little, except that all our dead, silenced by death, have fallen not into nothingness but into the loving embrace of God. And that's the only place where we can meet them, when we open our own hearts to the silent calmness of God's own self in which they now live. Not by selfishly calling them back to where we are, but by descending into the silent eternity of our own hearts where God abides in us, too.

We must not rush. Let us prefer to listen to the silence of inner grief, the silence in our own hearts and the silence of Holy Saturday, so that slowly, in faith, we can begin to feel the breath of the Holy Spirit breathing new life, breathing resurrection for Jesus and for our loved one who has died.

An unnamed Carthusian monk says that the experience of Holy Saturday is "passive." Why should our experience of grief not also be passive? Grief comes to us, we don't invite it! It confronts us with a vast empty nothingness. The same monk continues: "The experience of death before the Father raised him is one of absence of life, solitude, of nothingness. We must know that there exists a Holy Saturday during which the passion of Good Friday seems without value and without hope. We must know how to hope in this desert which is the domain of death; how to be dead with the God who is dead in order to rise with the Lord of life. Let us not be afraid. Christ has defeated death. Christ is risen."

Larry Kaufmann, CSsR,
with acknowledgment to his confrere,
Anthony Kelly, CSsR

2

"Blessed Are They Who Mourn, for They Will Be Comforted"

My mother had an Advent death. A few days short of her ninety-fifth birthday, she died full of years as the world geared up for the Christmas festivities. As a priest I have been to my share of deathbeds and funerals, but it was in her death that I could best recognize the comfort promised in the beatitude, "Blessed are they who mourn, for they will be comforted" (Matthew 5:4).

When the experience of mourning is seen in the context of our faith, new insights into the comforting of God can help us read our experience in a fresh light.

Types of Mourning

Mourning is not limited to the experience of a death. There is a very healthy mourning over our mistakes and our sins. It is healthy in that it can steer us away from dangerous paths. This is a kind of mourning familiar to the Jews: "Have mercy on me, God, in accord with your merciful love; in your abundant compassion blot out my transgressions....Cleanse me...

that I may be pure; wash me, and I will be whiter than snow" (Psalm 51:3, 9).

Mourning over sin is sometimes described as compunction ("*penthos*" in Greek). Connected to the idea of "puncturing," compunction is a spiritual quality of being "pierced to the heart" due to the very existence of sin—one's own or others'.

It would seem that the outrage, shame, and sorrow that people feel at the clerical child-abuse scandals can give us another insight into mourning. We lament the loss of innocence, we lament the betrayal of trust, we lament the wound caused to the body of Christ and the scandal given to the "least brothers [and sisters] of mine" (Matthew 25:40).

Compunction is a spiritual form of mourning and is often accompanied by the gift of tears. The tears of all who are damaged by scandals (including the perpetrators) are part of the tears of the Church, the tears of Jesus.

Lamentation

The Jews give us a rich tradition of mourning. They not only mourned over sin, they mourned over the tragedies and adversities of life. They developed a religious literature of mourning—lamentation—which finds its highest expression in the Book of Job. In this type of literature, our Jewish ancestors give us a vocabulary in which to question God, to wrestle with the problem of evil, to rage and storm against injustice and, in so doing, not to lose our humanity.

Even when enjoying prosperity we are invited by the Hebrew Scriptures to probe the secret of life, never to be satisfied with the trivial or superficial.

But of course, it is in dealing with death that our Jewish heritage best prepares us for the revelation of God in Christ. For seven days, Jewish mourners could do no work. They could not wash or even wear shoes. They could not read the Scriptures (Torah), for that was a joy. They could not shave, travel, or do business. They could eat no flesh and drink no wine. At the end of the seven days, they had to go to the synagogue and appear before the congregation, whose members would greet them with the words, "Blessed are those who comfort the mourner."

Jesus Wept

It is immensely significant for us as Christians that Jesus himself mourned. When Jesus encountered the funeral procession of the son of the widow at Naim, "he was moved with pity for her" (Luke 7:13). When his friend, Lazarus, died, "Jesus wept" (John 11:35). Jesus lamented the fate of Jerusalem: "As he drew near, he saw the city and wept over it, saying, 'If this day you only knew what makes for peace'" (Luke 19:41–42).

These insights from our Jewish past and from the life of Jesus surely reenforce the truth that it is good to mourn and lament. It is not only natural but graceful to observe rituals of mourning, whether in prayer, in dress, food, or in the drawing-down of blinds. The Jesus who mourned taught that mourning can be blessed, that it can be an occasion of grace, and that those who mourn in the Lord will be comforted.

Precisely because Jesus has faced grief, then all who are in Jesus can find comfort in his way of dealing with grief. Because of the tears of Jesus, our tears can be comforting. Because of Jesus' great prayer of lament on the cross, "My God, My God, why have you forsaken me?" our lamentations take on a divine dimension. Because Jesus has faced the ultimate in his own feeling of God-forsakenness, our trials cannot destroy us. Mourning in him, in him we are comforted.

Jesus himself is the comfort of those who mourn. In his own mourning he has drawn the sting out of our suffering: "Where, O death, is your victory? Where, O death, is your sting" (1 Corinthians 15:55)? His Spirit is at work in hearts broken by loss; his word steadies those left speechless with grief.

Some Helps

Mourning is obviously a process that takes its own course in each situation. While we can try and chart some broad guidelines, we cannot control its power and influence in our lives. But some indication can be set out that might help those who mourn to do so in Christ and thus come to some sense of the comfort of God.

1. **Accept the mourning process.** Mourning is the price we pay for loving. If we never loved, we would never have reason to mourn. Accept that mourning is good, indeed blessed. It raises our experiences of it to a new level.

2. **Enter into the rituals of mourning.** Every human culture surrounds the passing of a person with some rituals, often expressed in special prayers, special clothes, or signs of mourning, anniversaries, etc. These rituals humanize the raw emotions, allowing us to handle ourselves and our situation in creative and positive ways.

3. **Ponder your favorite passages of Scripture.** You could read the texts used at the funeral service or texts that have supported you in the past. Saint Paul wrote in his first letter to the Christians of Thessalonica that Christian mourning is quite different from the mourning of people "who have no hope." Reminding his readers that the death and resurrection of Jesus has changed our attitude toward death, he recommends that they should "console one another with these words" (1 Thessalonians 4:18). So we also should draw comfort from the word of God in the Scriptures.

4. **Revert to the simplest of prayers.** At times of acute mourning, we do not have the imaginative energy for long or intense forms of prayer. Mourners often find comfort in basic Christian prayers such as the Our Father, the Hail Mary, the Glory Be to the Father, a decade of the Rosary, or an invocation from our rich tradition: "Sacred Heart of Jesus I place my trust in you," or, "Jesus, Mary and Joseph, I give you my heart and my soul," or, "Eternal rest grant unto him/her O Lord." Often complete silence in the presence of God is best. Words can wear out or seem to

be drained of meaning, but silence before the mystery is always a restorative option.

It could only have been Jesus who saw me through the mystery of the death of my mother, a death so right at that age, a death so peaceful, and yet one that saw tears of sorrow transfigured.

Seán Wales, CSsR

3

Love
Never Ends

There is so little we understand about the afterlife or what heaven means. I don't think we are being honest if we delude ourselves that we have the answer to the question of what happens after death. Even the Christian faith does not give us precise answers about what happens after death. Paul writes that "eye has not seen, and ear has not heard...what God has prepared for those who love him" (1 Corinthians 2:9). The poet Percy Bysshe Shelley puts it in verse.

What is Heaven? a globe of dew
Filling in the morning new
Some eyed flower whose young leaves waken
On an unimagined world....

But while with all the best theology and philosophy we know less and less about heaven, one thing that just won't go away is a conviction about the eternal status of love. There is in us a powerful intuition, confirmed by the witness of the

Bible, that love conquers death; that "love is strong as death" (Song of Songs 8:6).

Christians are not really concerned with a life divided between this world and the next. We are concerned with one life, our new life in Christ and in the Spirit, the same life both now and after death. And that one continuous life is bound by one reality only: Love! As Paul writes in 1 Corinthians 13:8 (*New Revised Standard Version*), "Love never ends." Prophecy will fail, tongues will not continue forever, knowledge must fail. But, he says, "faith, hope, love remain, these three; but the greatest of these is love" (1 Corinthians 13:13).

Love never ends...but it does change, and its expressions change. During our life, our task is to see that love matures, grows, and develops. And in heaven, it is redeemed and purified—even more, it is given free reign—by being in the presence of God, who *is* love!

Love's Fulfillment

Death for a faithful Christian is the fulfilment of an earthly life of love. In death the love we have struggled to realize takes on a new dimension. It has not ended. It cannot end!

Again, the poet Shelley:

Music, when soft voices die,
Vibrates in the memory...
...And so thy thoughts, when thou art gone,
Love itself shall journey on.

I was blessed to have a cousin born with cerebral palsy. He had all the wonderful attributes that accompany that otherwise disabling condition. He had a love for life and a wide unconditional love for people. He died a week before his twenty-first birthday. We were overwhelmed by the crowds that attended his funeral, many of them complete strangers, like the street sweepers, the trash collectors, the postman, the milkman, the attendants at the local supermarket, and many others. All knew him, all loved him...and he loved them. I'll never forget a comment I heard: "We spend our lives struggling to love, or learning to love. He just loved!"

And his love has continued as people recall his memory and unite around stories of his life. It continues as family members invoke his intercession during exam times (he himself never passed a single grade!), or during travel or anything to do with cars (he loved cars, and told me he had already saved up more than five rands toward his first BMW!). It continued as his spirit "hovered" almost palpably during his mother's final hours, when it seemed as if he had come to fetch her. It may of course be asked if I am projecting my own wishful thinking here. Or is this what the continuity of love means, although we cannot fully grasp it or understand it?

We're back to our leading question: Can love come to an end? Can it die? With Paul we reassert our faith: "Love never ends!" Never! But is has to make transitions. Love has its own rites of passage. Getting married is one of them, having children another. But the final transition is death itself. Death is simply the transition of love. And heaven is the perfection of love, where, as we said, it is given free reign—because, after all, it has achieved total presence in the Reign of God, who *is* love.

Heaven

A word now about heaven. True, we did make the assertion that we know nothing about heaven, at least experientially. But God's revelation offers us a few pointers, the most graphic of which are to be found in the Book of Revelation. This book is not all gloom and doom! It does give us images of heaven and what we may anticipate, put together in the form of a huge collage, a mental painting of the future which is hidden as a small seed in our human history but which will be revealed as a pure gift of God. What are the main features of this collage?

1. **The future God offers is a "new creation."** There will be a new heaven and a new earth. What does that mean? In the first creation, we remember, God began his work by creating light. But night and darkness were still there. In the new future creation, light triumphs completely. There is no more night and darkness. And no more need for sun or moon. Everything is pure light. God himself is that light, and Jesus the Lamb is the lamp that lights everything.

2. **The future God offers is a "new paradise."** In the first paradise, there was a river that watered the garden. In the new paradise, the river rises from God's throne. It makes trees of life grow everywhere with leaves that are

the cure for the nations. This is an image that explains that death has been conquered. All that is left is life, life in abundance for everyone. The curse against reentering the first paradise has been lifted. There will be no more death, no more mourning or suffering.

3. **The future God offers is a "new covenant."** In the first covenant at Mount Sinai, God tells the Israelites: "I will be your God, you shall be my people." In the new covenant, God says he will make his home among us. His name is "God-with-us." And in the presence of God, we will be in perfect harmony with each other, where each one will be treated as a firstborn child.

4. **The future God offers is a "New Jerusalem."** Everything about it is perfect. The gates to the city are the Twelve tribes of Israel (the Old Testament). Its foundation stones are the Twelve apostles (the New Testament). Everyone contributes his or her wealth without losing anything in the process. There is no stinginess, only generosity.

5. **The future God offers is a people renewed and "beautiful as a bride."** The city of evil was a prostitute. The city of God is a bride. Her husband is the Lamb. The bride is the daughter of Israel, the image of the people of God. She is the woman who fought against death and the dragon. Here, in God's future, the struggle has ended. The serpent of the garden and the dragon of the Apocalypse are destroyed. All that remains is the wedding feast.

6. **The future God offers is God's self, "God-with-us."** Heaven has descended to earth. God has made earth his home. In John's Gospel, Jesus says: "Whoever loves me will keep my word, and my Father will love him, and we will come to him and make our dwelling with him" (John 14:23).

People generally find the Book of Revelation difficult to understand. But we must remember its author is using language and imagery of his time that have the basic purpose of making a sort of collage of what the future has in store for us. Behind that is a deeper purpose: to keep hope alive in the hearts of Christians who struggle and suffer for their faith.

Hope for the future has a direct bearing on how we live our lives today. My grandmother used to say, "There will be no criticizing in heaven, so you might as well start practicing now!"

So when we say love is eternal, maybe it is not that the love begun here on earth continues in heaven. Maybe it is the eternal power of love from a heavenly starting point (God's own love) that reaches into our temporal existence and gives us a taste of what is to come. It is the very life and love of God through Jesus Christ. "Whoever believes in the Son has eternal life" (John 3:36). They have passed from death to life. The Holy Spirit acts with great power to draw us into the life of God through Christ.

An Image of Life in God

Saint John of Damascus (675–749) has a wonderful image for the inner life of the Trinity stretching out to us humans and drawing us into their life of love. He assigns to this image the Greek word "*perichoresis*." That word is not difficult to understand, as we have two English words derived from its component parts: "peri-" meaning "around" (as in "peri-urban"); and "choresis" can be identified in our English word "choreography," which is the study and design of dance. So "*perichoresis*" simply means a circle dance, where John Damascene imagines the Father, the Son, and the Holy Spirit in a dance of love, opening up the circle and drawing us in. (I experienced this sort of thing when Zulu parishioners dancing in a circle insisted that I not be a mere onlooker. They actually hauled me into the circle!)

Heaven as a dance? Well why not? John, in the Book of Revelation, likens heaven to a wedding banquet. And what would a wedding be without dancing?

When do we take the first faltering steps in that dance? We take them in baptism when we are plunged into the paschal mystery of Christ. We take these steps as we begin our journey of discipleship, following in the steps of Jesus.

And the wedding dance is sustained most of all in the Eucharist, itself a banquet, in our communion with Christ.

If "love never ends," then we actualize that truth in a life of humble Christian service to others; and we celebrate it sacramentally in the Eucharist and, indeed, in all the other sacraments. At this point we would do well to reflect briefly on the meaning of a Requiem Mass—a Mass offered for a deceased person, usually at the funeral, although it may be repeated at an anniversary or for various pastoral reasons.

The Eucharist

Every Mass is a "memorial meal." Jesus said: "Do this in memory of me." Every Mass is a thanksgiving, a communion, a sacrifice, and an expectation of the coming of Christ. A Requiem Mass is a celebration of the way in which one who died in Christ shares these same realities. In a Requiem Mass we give thanks to God for the deceased person—and most of all for that person's life in Christ. Then we reaffirm our faith in the communion of saints—the fellowship that transcends the barrier of death. In a Requiem Mass we join the person to the self-giving offering of Jesus on the cross, praying with and in Christ for that person to also be able to say: Father, into your hands I commend my spirit. And finally in a Requiem Mass we rejoice that in Christ our brother or sister in Christ has gone "to prepare a place for [us]" (John 14:2). In fact, this idea of anticipation is expressed very well in the mystery of faith we proclaim, taken from the words of Saint Paul: "For as often as you eat this bread and drink the cup, you proclaim the death of the Lord until he comes" (1 Corinthians 11:26).

The Rolled-up Napkin

John's Gospel captures this "anticipation" in a powerful image: the head cloth neatly rolled up by itself in the tomb of the risen Lord (see John 20:7). Jesus knew what he was doing when he rolled up that cloth. He knew his disciples would have been aware of the common custom at that time when a landowner was at his meal. If he threw his napkin loosely on the table as he got up, the waiting servant would know he had finished his meal. If he neatly rolled up the napkin as he got up, the servant would know he was not finished yet and would come back. Jesus rolled up his head cloth! He was, in effect, saying, "I'll be back!"

As we commend our loved ones to God in the sure hope that we will meet again, we are actually releasing them into a greater capacity to love. This is a great consolation to us. It is rooted in our faith. It fills us with hope. And most of all, it reminds us again and again that love never ends.

Larry Kaufmann, CSsR

4

Living With Suicide

Death, no matter if it is expected or unexpected, always leaves us feeling defeated. The defeat is compounded considerably when the cause of death is suicide. When we face a suicide, we mourn the loss of someone, but we are also left with all the unanswered questions, as well as feelings of anger, the nagging second-guessing questions, and the anxiety and fear of the person's fate. I, as a priest, had to minister to others who had lost loved ones through suicide. Even though I tried to be as sensitive as possible, I never had to face the nagging questions until it happened to me.

My brother committed suicide.

On a cool, sunny June morning, as I was preparing to celebrate a wedding service, my phone rang. It was unusual for my father to be calling on a Saturday morning. As soon as I answered I knew something was wrong. He told me he had just found the body of my brother, who had committed suicide. This was the biggest shock of my life. In stunned silence I stared at the phone, thinking yet not thinking. I immediately needed to get into my car and drive across the city to make sure he wasn't wrong. When I arrived at the house, the flashing lights of emergency vehicles were sobering testimony that my father was not hallucinating. I made my way in through what seemed like crowds of emergency personnel and onlookers and went to his bedroom. There his body lay. He was indeed dead.

Words are not able to capture the plethora of thoughts and emotions I was plunged into. Why? How? Who should I phone? What must I do? It took five hours for police detectives to arrive and another two hours after their departure for the mortuary vehicle to collect his body. We lived at that scene for most of the day as his lifeless body lay in his bedroom. I still live at that scene in my memory, more alive than any other. It was, I think, the closest I have ever been to Good Friday. The words of the psalm that Jesus cried out from the cross are so poignant for me: "My God, my God, why have you abandoned me" (Psalm 22:2)? Where was God? How could God allow this to happen?

The days between my brother's death and the funeral were full of the business that inevitably accompanies death: planning a funeral, trying to get all his personal documents together, and dealing with various administrative processes.

Preparing a funeral for someone who has committed suicide is difficult. Inescapable questions linger in your mind: What will happen to him? How will God treat him? Which readings will be best? What does the Church say about suicide? What will people think? One unthinking woman had already told my mother that she was praying for his soul because of the terrible thing he had done to himself! Many other people tried to be of support and help; people I loved and ones I knew loved me. They tried hard to reach me, but I was somewhere else where they could not go. Some people got frustrated as they felt pushed away, but there are some things suicide does to you that you cannot explain, things you cannot understand until it has become part of you and your life experience.

During the days and months after the funeral there are many questions that just don't go away: the "why…" and "what if…" questions. Not only is somebody gone forever, but it is as if a part of you—a certain spark or joy—is lost, never to be recovered. Suicide robs you of something that words don't capture. It leaves a residue of pain and unanswered questions. There is little peace after suicide, and I came to understand that those who are left behind are victims of suicide as well.

Some Helpful Words

In a search for some degree of understanding, I came across some writing on suicide by Father Ronald Rolheiser, OMI, on his Web site. He said three things that I found most insightful and very helpful in dealing with suicide and, I think, making some peace with it:

1. Suicide is a disease; it is something that takes somebody out of this life against his or her will—the emotional equivalent of cancer, a heart attack, or stroke.

2. We, the loved ones who remain, should not spend undue time and energy second-guessing about how we might have failed that person, what we should have noticed, and what we might have done to prevent the suicide. Suicide is an illness and, as with a purely physical disease, we can love someone and still not be able to save him or her from physical death. God also loved this person and, like us, could not interfere with his or her freedom.

3. We shouldn't worry too much about how God meets a suicide victim on the other side. God's love, unlike ours, goes through locked doors, descends into hell, and breathes out peace where we can't. We can well imagine that the victims of suicide will awake on the other side to find Christ standing inside their locked doors, inside the heart of their chaos, breathing out peace and gently saying: "Peace be with you!"

Suicide Is Equivalent to a Disease of the Heart and Mind

Just as we can suffer from physical disease and our bodies eventually succumb to the disease—like cancer or HIV/ AIDS—so can our hearts and minds snap. Nobody chooses to die of cancer or AIDS. Suicide is a terminal illness just like other terminal illnesses. Nobody who is healthy wants to die, nobody who is healthy decides to commit suicide and burden their loved ones with their death. The person who commits suicide is a victim because he or she is too wounded, too raw, and too bruised to deal with the pain of life. As suddenly as a heart attack or stroke claims a life, so also does suicide. Rolheiser explains that the victim of suicide (in most cases) is a trapped person, caught up in a fiery, private chaos that has its roots both in his or her psyche and in his or her biochemistry. Suicide, in most cases therefore, is a desperate attempt to end unendurable pain, akin to one throwing himself off a high building because his clothing is on fire.

The emotional immune system of the suicide victim has shut down and, like cancer or any other disease, it is a horrible way to die. There is no freedom not to die. Suicide victims are, like victims of sickness and accidents, rarely responsible for their own deaths, and suicide should not be a matter of secrecy, shame, moral judgment, and second-guessing.

Could I Have Done More? What if...?

How could I have prevented this suicide? What should I have done better? Is it my fault? How did I fail this person?

These are the uncomfortable and painful questions that mourners face in the aftermath of suicide. They are troubling questions and leave feelings of betrayal and guilt. Insensitive friends and family members may blame each other for the death of a loved one.

I heard a story of a priest who told the parents of a young woman who committed suicide that they should go to the sacrament of reconciliation to ask forgiveness for driving their only daughter to suicide. I was indignant when I heard this because this attitude not only shows the priest's complete lack of understanding of human nature, but it also affirms the painful questions that suicide inevitably invokes. Pain, confusion, loss, and guilt are very real gut-wrenching feelings that those who are left behind have to navigate through. This may take years, maybe even the rest of our lives.

I met a woman who lost her son to suicide a few years ago. She was still struggling and very weepy as she spoke of her own pain. She was, she told me, continually overwhelmed by the unavoidable questions: How could I have prevented this? What difference would it have made if I was there? Rolheiser explains that we are not there at that moment precisely because the victim does not want us to be there. He or she chooses a time and spot when nobody is around. Suicide is a disease that picks its victim in a way that deliberately excludes others from being there. That is the anatomy of the disease.

To repeat, suicide is a sickness and, like many sicknesses, all the love and care in the world would not be able to cure it. This helps us approach those painful questions and feelings in a more balanced way. It should be an antidote against false guilt and endless second-guessing questions that compound the wound that suicide already leaves in our hearts.

Has My Loved One Gone to Hell?

The questions about the ultimate destiny of a loved one who commits suicide are perhaps the most haunting of all for those left behind. Not long ago the Church was unwilling to do the funeral of a suicide victim. A quick service in a side chapel or in the sacristy was the way it was awkwardly done. Suicide victims could not be buried in Church cemeteries.

In the Church we are embarrassed to say "suicide" or speak about it. Suicide has been called a "serious sin." This is a misunderstanding. It also exacerbates the situation and seems to assert that suicide victims are even beyond God's mercy. It reveals a deficient understanding of God. It plagues those left behind. Not only do we experience the powerlessness of the situation but what also seems to be the powerlessness and (possibly) the judgment of the Church.

In the aftermath of suicide we realize that the Church is limited, but God's reach is not. When we are helpless, when even the Church is helpless, we discover that God is not. The Apostles' Creed has a line that is filled with hope for those left behind after a suicide when it speaks of Jesus: "He descended into hell." There is no place where Jesus cannot go. When we cannot understand the inner chaos (the "hell") of loved ones, Jesus not only reaches out to them but chooses to descend into their hell. God can go to places we cannot, God has a depth of compassion and understanding that is infinitely wider and deeper than ours.

Rolheiser describes the suicide victim as one who is locked in the upper room of fear and pain, like the disciples after the death of Jesus. He says that it is only Jesus who can move through their locked door of unbearable pain and, in the midst of their soreness and fears, gently breathe new life into them and say, "Peace be with you." God can go to the furthest corners of the heart, the places no amount of good-will, love, therapy, or professional help on our part can reach, and breathe in peace and new life. It was Jesus' breath and message of peace that freed the disciples from their prison of fear after his death. It is this breath of new life and gentle words of peace that will free any of our loved ones who have been the victims of suicide.

We should not be worried about how God deals with those who suffer. God, in Jesus, shows special affection for those who suffer. Jesus chose to be with those who experienced their own brokenness and pain. Our loved ones who die through suicide are with the risen Jesus because he chooses to be with them. When all else seems to have failed and we are left in the hands of powerlessness, pain, and confusion because of our inability to respond in any way, it is he who descends into their hell and raises them up.

Those whom we love and whose lives have been claimed by suicide are living free of the emotional and mental pain they experienced on this side of heaven. They are living in God's loving embrace. They are filled with great joy and wholeness—the joy and wholeness we still long for. They have experienced, more than us, the healing love of God. They, in the desert of their pain, have cried out to the Lord and have been comforted by Yahweh. "I, the LORD, am your healer" (Exodus 15:26).

What About Us?

Perhaps the truth is that it is harder for us than for them now. We, too, need healing. We, too, need to feel the loving embrace of God. The words we ought to allow ourselves to hear now are the words that Jesus speaks to us who stay behind; to us who learn to live with suicide: "Do not let your hearts be troubled. You have faith in God; have faith also in me....I will come back again and take you to myself, so that where I am you also may be" (John 14:1, 3).

The prayer for the dead in the third Eucharistic prayer offers us consolation, a beautiful vision, and indeed tells us where our loved ones are now. It says, "There we hope to enjoy for ever the fullness of your glory, when you will wipe away every tear from our eyes. For seeing you, our God, as you are, we shall be like you for all the ages and praise you without end...."

Our loved ones so cruelly claimed by suicide wait for us to join them so that with them we can see God's glory and praise him forever. They are in the very glory of God. We can therefore take comfort that they are indeed well and truly in the presence of God. The words of the English mystic Julian of Norwich should comfort our hearts and help us to live longing to see our loved ones free from the abyss they once inhabited: "And all shall be well. All manner of things shall be well."

Russell Pollitt, SJ

Reflection After a Suicide

N. [insert name], we would like you to know that we miss you and that so much has changed because of you. We always thought this sort of thing happened to other people, not us.

Maybe, in your heart, you thought you were solving the problems you experienced or doing us a favor by taking your life. What hurts most is that we never were able to say, "Goodbye." You did not give us a chance to say, "Goodbye."

We have cried as we tried to understand your despair.

At times we have been angry with you for what you did to yourself, for what you did to us. At times we felt responsible for your death. We have searched for what we did or failed to do, for the clues we ignored or missed.

We feel the guilt of responsibility, of failure to keep you alive.

Yet we know that we didn't choose for you. If we were responsible for you, you'd still be alive.

We think of you so often, even when it hurts to remember. We are really lonely for your presence, and whenever we hear the words you spoke, we still cry for you. We feel sad that you're not here to share so many joyful moments with us.

That's when our mornings have no beginning and our nights seem as long as winter.

We try to remember the good times. Maybe you've seen us smile a little more.

We are learning to live again, realizing that we cannot die because you died.

We pray that you are at peace.

At the end of our days, we look forward to being with you again.

We miss you.

We really miss you.

5

Death and Forgiveness

The Stories of Etty Hillesum and Christian de Chergé

One of the harsh realities of living in South Africa (and indeed in any part of the world where crime and violence are common) is that we too often experience how an innocent life can be tragically and mercilessly snuffed out by a ruthless act. The reflection that follows is in no sense an attempt to rationalize what in fact cannot be rationalized, nor is it designed to lessen a type of grief for which there are, in fact, no words. Nevertheless, we cannot brush this type of grief aside, especially since it is usually accompanied by two things: (1) questioning God, and (2) feelings of hatred and revenge.

The approach taken in this reflection thus will not be philosophical. It will not try to explain the mystery of innocent suffering or the existence of evil. For most people, that is a futile exercise anyway. Rather, it will adopt a "narrative" style. It will tell the stories of two people who, in very different circumstances, grappled with the same challenges, particularly facing the temptation to be revengeful, and how they overcame that.

The two people in whose company we will be sitting and praying for a while are Etty Hillesum and Christian de Chergé. Etty Hillesum was a Dutch Jew from Amsterdam executed in the gas chambers of Auschwitz, and Christian de Chergé was a Trappist monk killed by Muslim extremists in Algeria. Let's get to know them now individually.

Etty Hillesum

The simple message of this twenty-seven-year-old woman is that the most helpful way to deal with the horrors of war and violence is to put yourself in solidarity with all who are suffering, not to hug your grief selfishly to yourself but to expand your heart to share in the experience of others who are in the same position. But what is remarkable about Etty's story is that she calls for sharing even in the grief of the "enemy!"

Etty kept a diary. They were eight exercise books closely written in small, hard-to-decipher handwriting, found only as recently as 1981. The diaries cover the years 1941 and 1942: years of war and oppression in Holland. But for Etty, it was a time of deep personal growth and personal liberation—growth and liberation that were the fruit largely of an extraordinary embrace of the gift of self-knowledge and a unique spirituality.

We do not know much about the details of Etty's life before the war. Born January 15, 1914, Esther "Etty" Hillesum came from a highly intelligent family. Her father, Dr. Louis Hillesum, taught classical languages, and her brother, Mischa, was a brilliant musician, considered to be one of the most promising pianists in Europe. Etty herself was a scholar of the Russian language and an official translator. At school she was known to be quite a bookworm, having a passion for philosophy and psychology. In this regard, she fell under the influence of Julius Spier, a protégé of Carl Jung.

As the persecution of Jews intensified, Etty's non-Jewish friends attempted to kidnap and hide her. But she was determined to share the fate of her fellow Jews and her family. She knew that the trains, each leaving with 1,000 Jewish prisoners, would pour their "cargo" out into total destruction, although she knew no details about gas chambers. She joined her family in the deportation order signed for September 7, 1943. The journey lasted three days. As she passed the Dutch border, Etty threw a post card from the window. It was picked up by local farmers and posted to her friend, Christine van Nooten. It said they left the camp singing. Her parents were sent to the gas chambers on the day of their arrival in Auschwitz. Etty met her fate on November 30, 1943. Her brother died the following March.

These are about the only externals we know of Etty's life. But through her diaries we literally learn volumes about her inner life. It is the life she reveals in her diaries where she records her daily experiences and her interior responses to them. The real interest of her diaries lies in the gentle mind that wrote them and in the astonishing internal journey that they represent. Etty is an example of the truism that the only spiritual life is life itself, in all its ambiguity and pain. As Etty explores the maze of relationships with friends, family, colleagues, and eventually with her Nazi captors; as she analyzes her often restless moods and feelings; as she shares in her diaries her thoughts about the growing evidence of disruption in the world at war around her, we see emerging a woman who once described herself as someone who refused to kneel but who now has abandoned herself into the arms of the God of life and love.

Out of this growing spirituality, in the short space of two years, we discover a woman transformed from an initial preoccupation with herself to an attitude toward life that is best described as "radical altruism," or as we say, "putting others first." In the last entry in her diary, written from the Dutch transit camp of Westerbork—where she spent all her energies encouraging her fellow Jews—she said we should be willing to act as a balm for all wounds. Etty's search for what is truly human stood in dramatic opposition to the inhumanity all around her.

Yet for Etty, her inspiration was no mere humanistic philosophy. It was rooted in God and in her life in God. She said there was a deep well inside her where God dwelled and where she sometimes lived. But more often, she said, God was "buried beneath stones" and must be dug out.

This takes practice. Etty was quite pragmatic about that. And so she said that sometimes the most important thing in a whole day is the rest we take between two deep breaths, or the turning inward in prayer for five short minutes. For her, striving for real interior freedom was slow and painful, and that we must be still and allow our inner selves to be at the service of others.

But what moves me most about Etty Hillesum is the profound connection she makes between her solitude—her inner life—and the war raging all round her, which forms her outer life. Jews may no longer visit grocer shops; they have to hand in their bicycles; they may no longer travel by tram and must be off the streets by 8 p.m.

In describing the feeling, Etty said the threat and terror from the Nazis was growing greater. She used prayer as a wall, withdrawing inside it before stepping outside and feeling calmer, stronger, and more collected.

And as the day approaches when she will be shipped off to Westerbork, the transit camp for Dutch Jews *en route* to Auschwitz, she digs deeper into the well. She said if your inner life is rich, the difference between the outside and inside of a concentration camp probably isn't all that great. She had few illusions. She knew life would be very hard, that she and her fellow Jews would be ripped apart from their dear ones, and that they would have to get even tougher within themselves.

As Etty makes the journey inward, into the depth of her soul where God dwells, she finds the strength to carry on. But the inner landscape also reveals to her that there is not much difference between the war outside and the war within. It was a Thursday evening, and the war was being waged outside her window, with exploding bombs lighting up the night sky. She lay there watching it all from her bed, and then suddenly it came to her that all disasters come from us. In wondering why war exists, she speculated that it might stem from her snapping at her neighbor due to her and her neighbor's lack of love. In fact, she said, no one has enough love.

For Etty, there is only one solution: to enter into complete solidarity and empathy with others, even with the enemy, the Nazi Germans, to take their sufferings into herself. She wants to be a balm for *all* wounds.

It is the story that follows that for me is the whole point of this reflection on her life. While on her way to the concentration camps, Etty delivered a message that echoes the mystery of our redemption in Jesus Christ: "Father, forgive them, they know not what they do." In this story, we may just find a spark of light and insight that could help us face the harsh reality of the violent death of a loved one.

Etty said it was important that we sometimes allow ourselves to feel truly sad. She said she believed that one day she would be able to say to her friend, Ilse Blumenthal, that life is beautiful, and that she values it daily, even while knowing that sons of mothers like Ilse were being killed in concentration camps. She urged Ilse to bear her sorrow, even if it seemed to be overwhelming. She assured Ilse that she would be able to arise again because people are strong. Further, she emphasized that Ilse's sadness must become part of her body and soul. Don't run from it, Etty told Ilse, but bear it like a grownup.

Continuing her message to Ilse, Etty urged her not to get caught up in hatred toward anyone, including German mothers, who also were sad because their sons have been murdered. Instead, Etty advised Ilse, give sadness all the room it needs, because if everyone bore her sorrow with honesty and courage, the great grief that filled the world would subside.

If you don't leave room for sadness, Etty argued to Ilse, and instead fill that inside space with thoughts of hate and revenge—which will only spawn new sadness for others—then sadness will never go away. In fact, she said, it will grow. But, she concluded, if you allow sadness the room it requires, you may ultimately say with conviction that life is beautiful; so beautiful that you cannot help but want to believe in God.

Christian de Chergé

On May 21, 1996, seven Cistercian monks from the Abbey of Tibhirine, Algeria, were assassinated by Islamic extremists. The whole community of monks had lived through terrible times of fear and violence but had decided as a group to remain in their monastery as a sign of love and hope for the Algerian people. Seven of them had been abducted in the early hours of the morning of March 27 and had been held captive for nearly two months. Their brutal murder shocked the world.

In the days following their execution, it emerged that the whole community had been very much aware of what might happen to them. In their journals and notebooks we can read how these men of God faced death well in advance. In particular, the superior of the community, Father Christian de Chergé, age 59, left a testament that has become something of a classic piece of spiritual writing. Father Christian reveals how he faced a violent death, how he integrated that death into his spiritual life, how he prayed for, and, in a sense, *with* his murderer.

The most radical statement of all and the one which logically led to his courageous decision to stand firm in his faith was that:

If it should happen one day—and it could be today—that I become a victim of the terrorism which now seems ready to engulf all the foreigners living in Algeria, I would like my community, my Church, and my family to remember that my life was given to God and to this country.

But he adds something quite profound. He shows an extraordinary humility by refusing to put all the blame for evil deeds on others, even the one he knows will slay him. He recognizes the power of evil within his own heart:

I have lived long enough to know that I am an accomplice in the evil which seems, alas, to prevail in the world, even in the evil which might blindly strike me down.

This insight into the mystery of evil and our part in everyone's sin leads to a profound compassion for the sinner. In his testimony, Father Christian prays:

I would like, when the time comes, to have a moment of spiritual clarity which would allow me to beg forgiveness of God and of my fellow human beings, and at the same time forgive with all my heart the one who will strike me down.

Father Christian's testimony then reveals how he faces death. He almost looks forward with curiosity and longing to see the face of God.

This is what I shall be able to do. Please God, immerse my gaze in that of the Father to contemplate with him His children of Islam, just as he sees them, all shining with the glory of Christ, the fruit of His Passion, filled with the Gift of the Spirit whose secret joy will always be to establish communion and restore the likeness, playing with the differences.

Toward the end of his testimony, Father Christian has words of thanks to God, to his friends and family and, most remarkably, to the one who will kill him: *To you, my last-minute friend, who will not have known what you were doing.* He can thank his murderer, "because in God's face I see yours." He can thank his murderer because in his humility he recognizes that both his murderer and he himself are sinners (he calls them both "*happy thieves*") who will meet again in paradise.

Hearing about how Father Christian and his monks faced death might seem very exceptional, heroic, and even mystical. To some it might seem naïve or idealistic. The reality is that we live in a violent society; we all know of individuals and even families devastated by barbaric cruelty.

While we pray not to be victims of violence and cruelty, we must face the truth that there are no exceptions to the universal law of death. But for Christians, as for those monks in Algeria, there is a power at work that carries them through everything: the power of God's Spirit in Jesus. To the Romans, Paul wrote, "If we live, we live for the Lord, and if we die, we die for the Lord; so then, whether we live or die, we are the Lord's" (Romans 14:8).

Conclusion: Facing Violent Death

The stories of Etty Hillesum and Christian de Chergé are exceptional and quite heroic. But perhaps we ourselves could have the courage at least to adopt them as models and as friends in the communion of saints to help us in our struggle in dealing with the kinds of death that result from evil acts.

For Etty, it meant solidarity with other mothers—even the mothers of the enemy—who also grieved. It meant trying to make herself a balm for others' wounds, reaching out in empathy rather than clinging selfishly to her own pain.

For Christian de Chergé, it meant following Jesus even in "loving your enemy," as he not only forgave his assailant but even called him his "last-minute friend" who was sending him to God.

Once again, we are not trying to rationalize death, especially violent death. All we want to do is to find some spark of faith, some example of love and forgiveness that may help us face a tragic death with hope and even, as Father Christian said, with joy. As he wrote to his parents:

I thank God, who seems to have willed it entirely for the sake of that joy in everything and in spite of everything.

In the evening of our life, we shall be judged only by love. There is no doubt that as Etty Hillesum and Christian de Chergé entered paradise they were judged by their extraordinary love, a love that began and ended in the God to whom they had given their lives.

Larry Kaufmann, CSsR, on Etty Hillesum
Seán Wales, CSsR, on Christian de Chergé

6

Augustine's Tears

The Death of His Mother

Saint Augustine is one of the great doctors of the Church, frequently referred to as an authority by theologians and scholars. But that will not be our concern here. This reflection looks at the human heart of Augustine, a heart that wrote the most profound "Confessions" in the history of literature, a heart that could overflow in copious tears of grief at the loss of a loved one.

Augustine was born in North Africa in 354 of Patricius and Monica. His famous baptism in Christ occurred in 387, for which he gives much credit to the prayers of his mother, Monica. The year after his conversion, Monica died. In his *Confessions*, Augustine describes the circumstances of her death, and he writes movingly about his grief.

> *Not long before the day on which she was to leave this life—you knew which day it was to be, O Lord, though we did not—my mother and I were alone, leaning from*

*a window which overlooked the garden in the courtyard
of the house where we were staying at Ostia.*

In these opening lines, Augustine acknowledges our human powerlessness before the mystery of death: "...you knew which day it was to be, O Lord." How important it is to entrust "the day and the hour" to God alone!

Augustine continues:

"I believe that what I am going to tell happened through the secret working of your providence. For we were talking alone together and our conversation was serene and joyful, 'forgetting what lies behind but straining forward to what lies ahead'" (Philippians 3:13). "In the presence of Truth, which is yourself, we were wondering what the eternal life of the saints would be like, that life which 'eye has not seen, and ear has not heard, and what has not entered the human heart'" (1 Corinthians 2:9).

Being Prepared

Could it be that Monica had a premonition that her days on earth were short? Did she want to prepare her son for her death? Many of us can no doubt give similar examples of parents, directly or indirectly, preparing us for their final departure. My own ailing father used to discuss with me what I would have to preach at his funeral! In fact, he insisted that I be very brief. All I had to say, he instructed me, was: "Christ has died. This man died in Christ. Christ is risen!" His idea was that people could work out for themselves the implications of this basic message about a person who lives and dies in Jesus. My mother, who had had several severe asthma attacks during which she stopped breathing, told me that next time she did not think she would have the strength to put up a fight. In the conversation we had, I suppose in a sense I gave her "permission" to die. It was a great relief to her. A mother naturally wants to make sure her children will be OK with her death. Monica must have been having these thoughts as she and Augustine were chatting:

> *Our conversation led us to the conclusion that no bodily pleasure, however great it might be and whatever earthly light might shed luster upon it, was worthy of comparison, or even of mention, beside the happiness of the life of the saints. As the flame of love burned stronger in us and raised us higher towards the eternal God...thinking and speaking all the while in wonder at all that you have made.*

The Glory That Awaits Us

We detect here a certain tension, much like the one Saint Paul experienced. Monica and Augustine celebrate the wonder of creation and the beauty of this earthly life—even human love. But they know by faith that it cannot compare to the glory that God has prepared for those who love him. Monica seems to have caught a glimpse of that new life, because she tells Augustine:

My son, for my part I find no further pleasure in this life. What I am still to do or why I am here in the world, I do not know, for I have no more to hope for on this earth. There was one reason, and one alone, why I wished to remain a little longer in this life, and that was to see you a Catholic Christian before I died. God has granted my wish and more besides, for I now see you as his servant.... What is left for me to do in this world?

Five days later Monica fell ill with a fever, at times losing consciousness. Augustine and his brother, Navigius, sat at her bedside. At one point she woke up and said to them, who were speechless with grief, "You will bury your mother here." Augustine describes how he could not respond, so choked up was he with grief. But his brother urged her (as we would say today) to "hang on" until they got home to their own country. In response to this, Monica's most famous words:

It does not matter where you bury my body. Do not let that worry you! All I ask is that, wherever you may be, you should remember me at the altar of the Lord.

Communion of Saints

Monica was not only asking that they should continue to pray for her after she died. She was not merely concerned for prayers for the salvation of her soul. She was also, in effect, telling them that in the memento for the dead at Mass, she was coming into the closest possible relationship that characterizes the communion of saints. An item of the Creed, this communion refers to the bond that continues between the living and the "living dead." It is a bond that is most powerfully strengthened in the mystery of the Eucharist.

Allow me to share a personal lesson from my own mother's death. I had been preaching a mission in Durban, South Africa, and joined my mother one Sunday for lunch. After the meal, she told me to leave the dishes for her to wash, as I had to get back to the mission. The next morning I got an urgent phone call. My mother was found to have died in her sleep. I rushed over to her flat, where my sister and brothers were assembling. Her eyes were open, seemingly gazing at the crucifix and the picture of Our Mother of Perpetual Help. After some time of prayer we went into the kitchen to make tea. Yes, the dishes were all washed, as she had said, and put away. On the kitchen counter were two loaves of bread that my mother had baked the night before, the very night she had died in her sleep. We ate that bread and shared it with our visitors. It was as if my mother was offering a kind of communion meal and saying to us, "Even after I have died, I will continue to nourish you from the other side. Take and eat this bread in memory of me."

But let's return to Monica and Augustine as we conclude this meditation. Continuing with her insistence that it did not matter where she died or even where she was buried, Monica, with a glint of humor, speaks her final words as recorded by her son: "Nothing is far from God, and I need have no fear that he will not know where to find me when he comes to raise me to life at the end of the world." After this, Augustine writes: "And so on the ninth day of her illness, when she was fifty-five and I was thirty-three, her pious and devoted soul was set free from the body."

Wave of Sorrow

What follows in Augustine's *Confessions* is one of the most powerful descriptions of the experience of grief ever written. "I closed her eyes, and a great wave of sorrow surged into my heart." He writes of the great effort it took to hold back his tears as he forced himself to listen to a "more mature voice within," the voice of his heart that helped him to keep his "sobs in check." For Augustine, the "mature voice" is that of his Christian faith, as he goes on to say, "We did not think it right to mark my mother's death with weeping and moaning, because such lamentations are the usual accompaniment of death when it is thought of as a state of misery or of total extinction." But of course Augustine knew this was not the case with his mother, as he was convinced of her holiness of life and that she had not died "in misery."

Yet despite this faith, Augustine's grief is profound. He looks into himself and asks where it comes from. The answer is simple. It comes from the bond of life and love between himself and his mother, and he feels that bond now to be broken, "suddenly cut off," leaving a deep wound. Perhaps a little selfishly (quite natural under the circumstances for any son or daughter!) he writes: "It was because I was now bereft of the all the comfort I had had from her that my soul was wounded and my life seemed shattered, for her life and mine had been as one."

Monica's Funeral

Augustine then describes the funeral and his initial inability to cry, and then finally receiving the gift of tears:

When the body was carried out for burial, I went and returned without a tear. I did not weep even during the prayers which we recited while the eucharistic sacrifice of our redemption was offered for my mother and her body rested by the grave before it was laid in the earth, as is the custom there. With all my heart I begged you to heal my sorrow, but you did not grant my prayer.

On reflection, Augustine realizes that this was so that God might teach him a lesson—to be less selfish in his grief and more grateful for all that his mother had been and done for him.

Then little by little, my old feelings about your handmaid, my mother, came back to me. I thought of her devoted love for you and the tenderness and patience she has shown me, like the holy woman that she was. Of all this I found myself suddenly deprived, and it was a comfort to me to weep for her and for myself and to offer my tears to you for her sake and for mine. The tears which I had been holding back streamed down, and I let them flow as freely as they would, making of them a pillow for my heart. On them it rested, for my weeping sounded in your ears alone.

Augustine then says something quite amazing. He says his tears have come as a gift to remind him of the tears his mother had shed over him for the debauched life he had led, and how she had wept before God so that Augustine should be converted. It's almost as if Augustine realizes for the first time what his mother had meant to him: If this is the pain I feel at her death, imagine how much pain she had felt at my sinfulness.

Remembrance at Mass

In this sense, grief is a necessary aspect of continuity in a relationship in the communion of saints. It deepens our appreciation of the person who has died, it helps us understand things we had not realized before, and it takes us onto a new and more mature level of personal growth. Once again, the most important place for this to be experienced is in the Eucharist. Offering Masses for the dead—and being present when that intention is offered—is no idle exercise. It is truly an act of faith in the continuity of a relationship in Christ (who is the same yesterday, today, and forever) between ourselves and our deceased loved ones. This is something that "money can't buy," as the saying goes—not the best coffins nor the most elaborate tombstones. It is to this same theme that Augustine returns as he concludes his account of his mother's death and his ensuing grief, repeating similar words but expanding on them:

My mother had no care whether her body was to be buried in a rich shroud or embalmed with spices, nor did she wish to have a special monument or a grave in her own country. These were not the last wishes she passed on to us. All she wanted was that we should remember her at your altar, where she had been your servant day after day without fail. For she knew that at your altar we receive the Holy Victim in whom we have triumphed over the enemy, even the last enemy called death.

Augustine ends with a dramatic insight, which can only come from faith in Christ, our firstborn brother:

Let her rest in peace with her husband....They were not only my parents on this earth, but they were also my brother and sister, subject to you, our Father, in our mother the Church, and they will be my fellow citizens in the eternal Jerusalem for which all your people sigh throughout their pilgrimage, from the time when they set out to the time when they return to you.

Larry Kaufmann, CSsR

7

The
Bereaved Child

1. **The bereaved child needs to talk.** Adults are often at a loss about how to deal with a bereaved child. There is a tendency to keep grieving children occupied and out of the way when, in fact, the greatest need is for them to talk about their sense of loss and their real sadness. For a child, the first step in mourning is to talk.

2. **The bereaved child needs to mourn.** No less than an adult, a child has to mourn and, even unconsciously, process the loss that has occurred. The sensitive adult will not shield the child from the mourning process but will look for appropriate ways for the child to express the feelings that are being experienced.

3. **The bereaved child needs to cry.** It can be very helpful for an adult to weep with the child, thus giving the child a sense of the rightness of tears while doing so in a context of privacy and security. The gift of tears in this context can be explained to the child as a sign of love as

well as of loss, an experience that can help anyone cope with death.

4. **The bereaved child needs to pray.** Death is a profoundly religious experience. It is important for the child to be helped to connect this experience with the life of the Spirit. God remains the Good Shepherd both of the living and the dead. Even very simple prayers for a lost parent or sibling can keep the experience from becoming hopeless for the youngster.

5. **The bereaved child needs ritual.** If a child is old enough to go to Mass, it can be a positive aspect of mourning for the child to attend the funeral. By attending the funeral, the child can be given a strong sense of belonging and of being important to the family during a critical time. The child can be afforded an opportunity to participate in an appropriate way in the funeral rites.

Seán Wells, CSsR

8

Reconciliation Beyond the Grave?

A Healing Meditation

The title of this reflection has a question mark after it. It asks whether it is possible for there to be reconciliation with someone after he or she has died. This question applies to situations where there had perhaps been some estrangement or conflict at the time of death, especially when that death was sudden and unexpected.

This is not uncommon, and those left behind are often burdened with feelings of remorse, guilt, and regret. But in our life of faith this should never be the final word. Jesus has achieved perfect reconciliation. That reconciliation "is finished" on the cross (John 19:30). It is reconciliation between us and God, and between one another. Yet how do we realize it, or experience it, when there was a breakdown in a relationship at the time of someone's death?

The first thing to be recommended is to find reconciliation in and through the Mass. It is in the Eucharist that we experience most fully and sacramentally the communion of saints—the communion and ongoing fellowship that exists between the living and the "living dead"—those who have died to this world but are living already in the world to come. Christ is the same yesterday, today, and forever, and in Christ we find our communion—our reconciliation—with one another. Practically, in this light, it is helpful to have a Mass said for the deceased person and during the Mass to ask one another forgiveness for past hurts and conflicts.

On a more personal, and, to some extent, psychological level, the following meditation may be helpful. It is based on the story of the two disciples on the road to Emmaus. Their hopes had been dashed with the death of Jesus. They were going home, disillusioned and depressed. For them, all was lost. But an extraordinary encounter with Jesus takes place, and their faith and hope are renewed. Perhaps begin the meditation by reading the full text from Luke 24:13–35.

Now enter into a quiet time of imaginative meditation using the following steps. Start by invoking, in your own words, the wisdom and light of the Holy Spirit.

1. Be alone. Invite quiet into your heart and spirit.

2. Imagine the Emmaus road through the Judean countryside where the two disciples walked, conversing. They are depressed, discouraged, dejected.

3. Now imagine that you are one of those two disciples. The other person with you is the deceased person whom you have hurt or who has hurt you.

4. Have an imaginary conversation in which you speak honestly with the other about what had happened, how you each feel. Do not shy away from unpleasant or angry feelings or the pain of memory. Make sure you give each other equal time to speak. (If you knew the other well, you would know what he would say.)

5. Jesus comes along and joins you in your walk. He asks you: "What are you discussing as you walk along" (Luke 24:17)? You tell him honestly.

6. What does Jesus say? Allow Jesus to speak to the situation.

7. Now you reach an intersection on the road. Jesus tells you he is taking the other person along with him, but that you must remain behind for the time being, going your own way. Jesus embraces you. The other person embraces you. Watch them walk off and fade into the distance.

8. Reflect on the words of the text from Luke: "Their eyes were opened and they recognized him, but he vanished from their sight" (Luke 24:31). Bring your meditative dialogue to the Mass or to a time of adoration before the Blessed Sacrament. (Perhaps here arrange to have a Mass intention offered for the deceased person.)

Larry Kaufmann, CSsR

9

The Book of Job
and the Stages of Grief

Perhaps the most well-known contemporary writer on death and dying is Elisabeth Kübler-Ross, MD. After many years of working with terminally ill patients and dealing with families after a death, she found that a common pattern emerged. This led her to describe the process of dealing with death, both in the patient and in mourners, in five stages. These are (1) denial, (2) anger, (3) bargaining, (4) depression, and (5) acceptance. Of course, these stages can occur on the same day, or they can occur over a period of time within the total process. In one day we can find ourselves fluctuating between feelings of anger, depression, or acceptance. Over a much longer period, there are dominant phases where, through a process of inner reflection or simply allowing nature to take its course, we "mature" from initial denial to courageous acceptance.

There is, of course, a danger of taking Kübler-Ross' stages and turning them into a set program. Ellen Goodman wrote an interesting article in *The Boston Globe* titled, "Let's Stop the Jargon of Efficient Mourning." Goodman rejects the idea that death is something to deal with, that we're meant to get over a loss according to a prescribed emotional timetable. For Goodman, grief is as individual as the death and the mourner. But today there seems to be an approach that turns grief into a set process with rules that must lead to closure. We have, in essence, says Goodman, tried to make grief into a science. But in real lives, she adds, each person has his or her own grief timetable. If anything, it may often be an ongoing lifelong process that one never closes.

Goodman says that even though we seem to have a penchant for doing things fast and efficiently, grief has its own clock, and it lies within each individual's heart. And when you lose someone, especially someone close, that clock will run down in its own good time.

Kübler-Ross would not disagree. Her five stages are simply pointers to help us be in touch with the variety of feelings that churn around in our human hearts. Even the final stage of "acceptance" is bittersweet. It does not mean that the pain of grief simply goes away. The scar of loss will and must remain, even as the risen Jesus showed his disciples the wounds that caused his own death. Indeed, long after we accept a person's death, we experience moments of memory that rekindle feelings of grief.

Elisabeth Kübler-Ross has helped many people on the road of bereavement, providing useful signposts along the way. The question I want to ask is, does the Bible offer a similar aid? It does. It is found in the story of Job, that "patient" man (although not always!) who lost everything: children, livestock, and all his possessions.

The theme of the Book of Job is summarized in the question: *Why do bad things happen to good people?* And it asks this question as a challenge to the popular belief that sin leads to suffering, and virtue leads to worldly reward. So if Job lost everything, he must have sinned. That is the theology his three visiting friends kept pumping into him. But Job, like a typical South African, says: Ja/Nee! Yes…but no! His experience teaches him something else: the possibility of innocent suffering, and the problem of how we are to talk *about* God and *to* God in the face of it.

This is where we also find in Job various stages of insight and growth in wisdom.

Popular Sayings

After his initial loss, he starts by using the language of popular faith. In other words, he falls back on the sort of slogans we find on bumper stickers or hear spouted by some televangelists: "Relax, God is in charge!" So Job's initial response would have been to quote a popular slogan: "Naked I came forth from my mother's womb, and naked shall I go back there. The LORD gave and the LORD has taken away" (Job 1:21). Or again, "We accept good things from God; should we not accept evil" (2:10)? This kind of language gives a little comfort at first, but it comes from common sayings, not from the depths of his heart.

Silence

And so Job decides to go silent (2:13—3:1). His friends join him in keeping silence. For seven days they remain silent. The intention of the friends is one of sympathy and consolation, and they begin by respecting that Job doesn't want to talk. What can one say in the face of terrible misfortune? We keep silent. There is a big difference between the language of the lips and mouth and the language of the heart (where we do not necessarily know the answers). Finally, Job breaks the silence and moves into a new phase.

Doubts and Questions

He starts to articulate his doubt and questions. He curses the day he was born. One after the other he challenges and even destroys the language of the slogans, the popular sayings. He does so because he asks the really tough question: Why? Why? Why? And the more Job questions, the more his friends feel free to give answers, all based on the traditional doctrine, supported by "divine revelation," and they tell Job that repentance will lead to restoration. But as they slow down with their speeches (and eventually Zophar drops out), Job just keeps going. He goes deeper with his questions.

Faith Seeking Understanding

Now his language becomes the language of theology. In Saint Anselm's definition, theology is simply "faith seeking understanding." It is not the same as catechism. It is not just repeating old doctrines, but rather trying to make sense of Scripture and the tradition, especially when the reality does not fit the theory. Job grapples with questions of what is true and false, what is deception and illusion, what is secret and hidden, what, in fact, is pure mystery. He avoids the temptation to twist reality to fit the theory. The friends with all the traditional answers eventually give up the debate, but the one who suffers (Job) does not give up. There is too much at stake for him. He has nothing to lose. But now that he no longer has his so-called "friends" to talk to (he has, in fact, lost patience with them), to whom does he talk? So from speaking *about* God, Job next moves on to speak directly *to* God.

Conversation With God

This is the essence of prayer. Saint Alphonsus Liguori describes prayer as "speaking continually and familiarly with God as to your dearest friend." Job thus prays: "Oh, that I had one to hear my case:...Let the Almighty answer me! Let my accuser write out his indictment" (31:35)! He demands a hearing from God. True prayer is completely honest with God, holding nothing back. We are starting to feel some progress. A direct dialogue between God and Job begins.

Ironically, God does not give direct answers. Instead, God speaks out of the heart of a massive storm, out of the grandeur of creation. God simply puts Job in his place as a creature. By teaching Job that he remains Job's Creator, and that Job in fact is a beloved creature of God, God brings Job to a stage of complete abandonment to God's providence and grace (42:1–6). Job spoke truthfully, and God commends Job for his honesty and fidelity.

Yes, God speaks through a person's immediate, lived experience, as painful as it may be. Thomas Merton even suggests that suffering, grief, and loneliness become God's shortcut to the soul. God rejects the wishy-washy theories of Job's friends who are so sure of themselves but fail completely as far as true empathy is concerned, and God declares Job to be his true friend. It's as if they have been through something together.

Many people have turned to the Book of Job in times of great suffering, loss, and bereavement. You may want to do the same yourself, and read it in full.

Also, you may want to use the meditation below, based on Elisabeth Kübler-Ross' five stages, and work through them at your own pace.

Healing of Grief

1. **Denial**
   Lord, let me see in myself the truth you see in me.

Where am I in denial? What do I refuse to consider? What do I refuse to see about the situation / the event / the death? What do I deny about my loss?

2. **Anger**
   Lord, comfort me in my pain.
   Help me not to take it out on you, or others,
   or even on myself.

Who am I blaming? How does my behavior become self-destructive? What do I wish could have happened differently? What am I feeling right now?

3. Bargaining

Lord, let me be open to all circumstances...unconditionally.
Let me see all from your point of view.

What conditions do I keep imposing? (These are the many "what ifs....") Do I keep putting off the moment of letting go (the "not yets")?

4. Depression

Out of the depths I cry to you, O Lord. You seem to have
forsaken me. Forgive me for not trusting you.

What past hurts dominate me? Where have I closed in on myself? Where am I refusing to build new bridges to others and to a new future for myself?

5. Acceptance

Lord, thank you. I am ready for all, I accept all.
Let only your will be done in me.
Into your hands I commend _____ (here add the name
of the person whose death you mourn).

Where has there been growth and transformation? How have I been healed? What hope have I found in my faith?

Larry Kaufmann, CSsR

10

Reflections and Prayers

Helping You Through the Grieving Process

Where There Is Hope

We may feel utterly lost, alone and isolated. We may even feel that God has abandoned us. We have believed in God, and now our faith seems empty. We need not fear, for God is with us in our need. We can be one with Christ our Lord as we pray for those we love. Ask the Lord to take care of them. We know that it is in him that we are each to find our peace. And as we pray for the one we love, we are confident that he hears our prayer. We discover the unity with Christ that endures all things.

It is no wonder that our Lord says to us, "Do not let your hearts be troubled. Trust in God still, and trust in me." He has prepared a place for us and for those we love. We may feel lost and full of anxiety at the moment when one we love has died. We are bereft and want to know what has happened to them. If we can pause and listen to the voice of God in our hearts, we may know that they are at peace.

FROM DEATH IS ONLY A HORIZON

> *"The souls of the righteous are in the hand of God, and no torment shall touch them. They seemed, in the view of the foolish, to be dead; and their passing away was thought an affliction and their going forth from us, utter destruction. But they are in peace."*

BOOK OF WISDOM 3·1–3

Grief

When we suffer a great loss, we are certain to be deeply sad. Our sadness may be painful to express. We may want to grieve but feel afraid. We may not want to show our feelings. We may feel we have to be strong for someone else's sake. But this is a time for grief. Jesus wept when his close friend died. And when he saw the grief of the sister of Lazarus, he grieved with her.

When we suffer a real loss, we may want to cry. It is a natural reaction. This is part of mourning, it is not a weakness or self-indulgence. It is the acknowledgment of loss. We each need to express our sadness in some way and to let those close to us share it with us. They also want to mourn and may need to weep. Each of us mourns in some way when one we love has died.

FROM DEATH IS ONLY A HORIZON

"When Jesus saw her weeping and the Jews who had come with her weeping, he became perturbed and deeply troubled, and said, 'Where have you laid him?' They said to him, 'Sir, come and see.' And Jesus wept. So the Jews said, 'See how he loved him.'"

JOHN 11:33–36

A Loved One Has Died

We give back to you, O God, those whom you gave to us. You did not lose them when you gave them to us, and we do not lose them by their return to you. Your dear Son has taught us that life is eternal and love cannot die. So death is only a horizon, and a horizon is only the limit of our sight. Open our eyes to see more clearly and draw us closer to you that we may know that we are nearer to our loved ones, who are with you, who are with you. You have told us that you are preparing a place for us: Prepare us also for that happy place, that where you are we may also be always, O dear Lord of life and death.

FROM *DEATH IS ONLY A HORIZON*

"Do not let your hearts be troubled. You have faith in God; have faith also in me. In my Father's house there are many dwelling places. If there were not, would I have told you that I am going to prepare a place for you? And if I go and prepare a place for you, I will come back again and take you to myself, so that where I am you also may be."

JOHN 14:1–3

In the Hands of God

All our lives we have known of God's love for us. Now, in our special need, that love is our refuge and strength. Think for a moment of what he has promised to those who love him. The kingdom of heaven is in our midst. Heaven is the fulfilment of all that we have hoped for and longed for: to find love and peace forever in Christ. This is the secret of happiness. Deep within our hearts we can find that love of God. This is the God who made all things, and he shares with us the love that made the world. All the good things we have known are from him. He has waited for us to complete our pilgrimage. We need not fear what he has in store for us. We know he made us for heaven to enjoy the embrace of our Father in the eternal family of God.

FROM *DEATH IS ONLY A HORIZON*

"My help comes from the LORD, *the maker of heaven and earth....The* LORD *will guard you from all evil; he will guard your soul. The* LORD *will guard your coming and going both now and forever."*

PSALM 121:2, 7–8

With Mary Our Mother

Mary stood at the foot of the cross as her Son died. His last words commended us to her care. This Mother suffered the darkness of grief when the dead body of Jesus was taken down from the cross. In our grief we can call on her, cry with her.

We may quietly stay with her in contemplation of the love that God has given us and that can never be taken from us. She is with her Son in glory now and is a sure sign of hope and comfort for every one of us.

FROM *DEATH IS ONLY A HORIZON*

"Standing by the cross of Jesus were his mother and his mother's sister, Mary the wife of Clopas, and Mary of Magdala. When Jesus saw his mother and the disciple there whom he loved, he said to his mother, 'Woman, behold, your son.' Then he said to the disciple, 'Behold, your mother.'"

JOHN 19:25–27

The Memorare

Remember,
O most gracious virgin Mary,
that never was it known, that anyone who fled
to your protection, implored your help,
or sought your intercession, was left unaided.
Inspired with this confidence, we fly unto you,
O Virgin of Virgins, our Mother.
To you do we come, before you we stand,
sinful and sorrowful.
O Mother of the Word Incarnate,
despise not our petitions, but in your mercy,
hear and answer us. Amen.

PRINTED IN *DEATH IS ONLY A HORIZON*

Adapted from the Preface for Christian Death I

Lord God, your Son Jesus Christ rose from the dead.
By his rising, our hope of resurrection dawned.
Help me, in this time of grief,
    to take comfort in the risen Jesus.
He shows us that the sadness of death gives way to the
    bright promise of immortality.
The risen Jesus assures us that life has changed, not ended.
When the earthly body lies in death we gain
    an everlasting dwelling place in heaven.
Be my confidence in this time of loss. Help me to feel the
    gentle support of Jesus,
    who by his rising has destroyed death forever.
Amen.

The home that you are going to…

And now, _____, go in peace,
There is no need to be afraid.
May there be a beautiful welcome for you
In the home that you are going to.
You are not going somewhere strange.
You are going back to the home that you never left.
You have lived your earth life to the full,
So may you live to the full, eternal life.
May those whose lives you touched on earth be blessed.
May you be peaceful and happy.
May your going be light and swift

And your welcome in heaven assured.
May your soul smile in the embrace of God.

BASED ON A CELTIC PRAYER

De Profundis ~ *Psalm 130 (129)*

Out of the depths I call to you, LORD;
LORD, hear my cry!
May your ears be attentive
to my cry for mercy.

If you, LORD, keep account of sins,
LORD, who can stand?
But with you is forgiveness
and so you are revered.

I wait for the LORD,
my soul waits
and I hope for his word.

My soul looks for the LORD
more than sentinels for daybreak.

More than sentinels for daybreak,
let Israel hope in the LORD,
For with the LORD is mercy,
with him is plenteous redemption,
And he will redeem Israel
from all its sins.

Prayer of a Mourner

Lord God, you watched as your Son Jesus died on the cross.
I watched as N. [insert name] left this world, too.
Be with me and all my loved ones who are grieving this loss
as we journey on together without N. [insert name].
Comfort us as we mourn, and help us to remember that we
    are not alone;
we have each other and we have you.
Grant us consolation and peace in the darkness of our grief.
    Amen.

Prayer After the Loss of a Baby

God of hope in our hopelessness,
God of power in our powerlessness,
God of strength in our weakness,
please be with me as my heart bleeds
    because of the loss of my baby.
Be with me in this time of pain and sorrow,
guide me through the darkness of anger and despair,
and remind me, through others around me,
that you have not forsaken me even though
    it may feel that way.
Bless and keep all who mourn their babies;
    that we may be comforted. Amen.

Prayer After the Death of a Child

O most sorrowful Mother, your only Son was called
    the fairest of all people.
You lost him in death on Calvary.
Mary, my child is gone now, too;
in this earthly life I shall never see my dear one again.
My heart is broken just as yours was broken.
Help me to know that my child, [insert name],
    is with yours.
Teach me, dear Mother,
how to live through the heartache and pain I feel
    at this terrible loss.
You have made this journey. Journey with me,
    I beg you now. Amen.

Prayer After the Death of a Parent

Lord God, you commanded us to honor
    our father and mother.
I commend my father/mother to you.
Look with compassion on him/her and forgive his/her sins.
May I come to see him/her again in the everlasting
    brightness of your Kingdom.
I give you thanks for the life that you gave to him/her,
    which was shared with me.
Help me in this time of mourning to feel your
    consolation and love.
I ask this through Jesus your Son and our risen Lord. Amen.

Prayer After the Death of a Spouse

O heavenly Father, I am now in the shadow
    of great loneliness.
My helpmate has left me.
I know that you love my spouse who, I pray,
is now in heaven rejoicing with you.
Grant me the strength I need to bear my present burdens,
and help me to look for opportunities to seek out those
    less fortunate than myself.
Keep me from feeling sorry for myself
    in my present condition,
and keep my heart inflamed with love for you and
    for my neighbor,
so that I can help to witness to your work of love
    in this world.
May I one day be reunited with my beloved spouse
    in heaven,
where we both can worship you for all eternity. Amen.

Prayer After a Suicide

Lord our God,
you are always faithful to us and quick to show mercy.
We pray for N. [insert name],
who was suddenly and violently taken from us.
We have so many painful questions Lord.
We cannot imagine the fiery pain and inner chaos
that he/she was feeling in his/her darkest time.
Come swiftly to his/her aid.
May he/she hear the gentle words of Jesus,
    "Peace be with you," at this time.
Grant him/her peace Lord, a peace that we could not give.
Comfort us who remain. Heal our pain.
Console us when the "whys" overwhelm us.
Help us to let go of the responsibility, guilt, and anger.
We ask this through Christ our Lord. Amen.

Prayer After a Violent Death

1.
Merciful God,
hear the cries of our grief,
for you know the anguish of our hearts.
It is beyond our understanding and more than we can bear.
Accept our prayer for N. [insert name],
as he/she has been released from this world's cruelty
so may he/she be received into your safe hands
    and secure love.

We pray that justice may be done
and that we may treasure the memory of his/her life
more than the manner of his/her death.
We ask this in the name of Jesus, our Lord,
who suffered the same violence and cruelty as N.
[insert name]. Amen.

Prayer After a Violent Death

2.
God of love,
we thank you that N. [insert name] is in your gentle
and loving hands,
far from the cruelty, violence and pain of our world.
When the trouble was near, we could not understand
how you seemed to remain far away.
And yet it is to you we turn;
for in life and death
it is you alone whom we can trust,
and yours alone is the love that holds us fast.
We find it hard to forgive the deed
that has brought us so much grief.
But we know that, if life is soured by bitterness,
an unforgiving spirit brings no peace.
Lord, save us and help us.
Strengthen in us the faith and hope that N. [insert name]
is freed from the past with all its hurt,
and rests forever in the calm security of your love and
in Jesus Christ our Lord. Amen.

Thanksgiving During Grief

God of power and might,
thank you for the joys I have experienced in my life
especially in the midst of the grief I now experience.
I rejoice that you continue to be with me
and let the light of your love shine on me so that my heart
     can be healed.
Bless and keep me
as I continue to seek new life through grief,
now and always. Amen.

Prayer to Let Go

Lord God,
My heart is broken by the death of N. [insert name].
I am finding it so hard to go about my daily tasks
     with such a heavy heart.
I cherish N. [insert name], but help me to realize
     that he/she is not my life.
I have my own gift of life to live.
Help me to let go so that I can live my life to the full and
     one day rest secure in your arms with N. [insert name].
I ask this in the name of Jesus our risen Lord. Amen.